How to use this book 

Follow the advice, in italics, where given.
Support the children as they read the text that is shaded in cream.
Praise *the children at every step!*
Detailed guidance is provided in the Read Write Inc. Phonics Handbook.
Activity 8 (Answer the 'questions to read and answer') only appears in Sets 4–7.

---

8 reading activities

Children:

1 Practise reading the speed sounds.
2 Read the green and red words for the non-fiction text.
3 Listen as you read the introduction.
4 Discuss the vocabulary check with you.
5 Read the non-fiction text.
6 Re-read the non-fiction text and discuss the 'questions to talk about'.
7 Re-read the non-fiction text with fluency and expression.
9 Practise reading the speed words.

Speed sounds

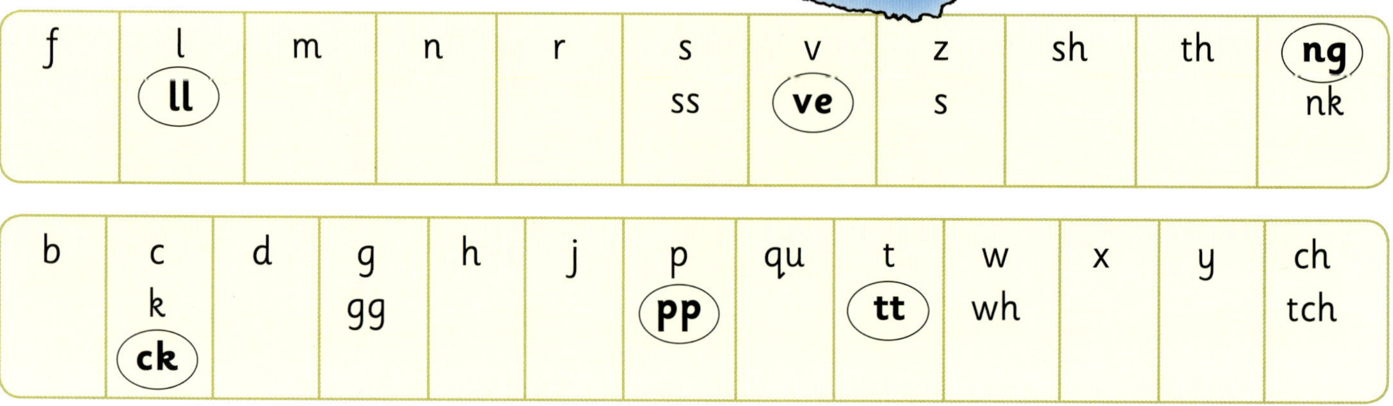

Consonants *Say the pure sounds (do not add 'uh').*

f	l / **ll**	m	n	r	s / ss	v / **ve**	z / s	sh	th	**ng** / nk

b	c / k / **ck**	d	g / gg	h	j	p / **pp**	qu	t / **tt**	w / wh	x	y	ch / tch

Vowels *Say the vowel sound and then the word, e.g. 'a', 'at'.*

at	hen	in	on	up	day	see	high	blow	zoo

*Each box contains one sound but sometimes more than one grapheme. Focus graphemes are **circled**.*

Read in Fred Talk (pure sounds).

felt   from   jump   lo<u>ng</u>   so<u>ck</u>

scrap   ha<u>ve</u>

Read in syllables.

pupp` et → pu<u>pp</u>et      Ja` pan → Japan

bu<u>tt</u>` on → bu<u>tt</u>on

Read the root word first and then with the ending.

hand → hands   stri<u>ng</u> → stri<u>ng</u>s   fix → fixed

<u>the</u>   <u>th</u>e<u>se</u>   <u>th</u> <u>ey</u>   <u>are</u>

<u>you</u>   of   <u>fing</u> <u>er</u>*

*red for this book only

Puppets

Introduction

Have you ever seen a puppet show?
What did you enjoy about it?
Have you ever played with a puppet?
This book shows you lots of
different puppets!

Written by Gill Munton

Vocabulary check

Discuss the meaning (as used in the non-fiction text) after the children have read the word.

<table>
<tr><td></td><td>**definition**</td></tr>
<tr><td>**Japan**</td><td>*a country in Asia*</td></tr>
<tr><td>**rod**</td><td>*a thin piece of wood or metal*</td></tr>
<tr><td>**scrap**</td><td>*something that is left over*</td></tr>
<tr><td>**felt**</td><td>*a type of soft material*</td></tr>
</table>

Punctuation to note:

Japan	*Capital letter for the name of a country*
Let's Pull	*Capital letters that start sentences*
.	*Full stop at the end of each sentence*
!	*Exclamation mark*
:	*Colon to show that a list is next*
•	*Bullet points for each item in a list*

You can have lots of fun with puppets!

String puppets

This is a
string puppet.

The puppet's hands and legs have strings.

Pull the strings and the puppets will run and jump.

Rod puppets

These puppets are fixed on long rods.
They are from Japan.

Hand puppets
This is a hand puppet.
14

It is:

- a sock

- 2 buttons

- a scrap of red felt.

Finger puppets

Ten puppets on ten fingers!

Questions to talk about 

Re-read the page. Read the question to the children. Tell them whether it is a FIND IT question or PROVE IT question.

FIND IT	PROVE IT
✓ *Turn to the page*	✓ *Turn to the page*
✓ *Read the question*	✓ *Read the question*
✓ *Find the answer*	✓ *Find your evidence*
	✓ *Explain why*

Page 11:	FIND IT	*What parts of the puppet's body are the strings attached to?*
Page 12:	FIND IT	*How do you make the puppet move?*
Page 13:	FIND IT	*Where are rod puppets from?*
Page 15:	FIND IT	*What do you need to make a hand puppet?*

Speed words

Children practise reading the words across the rows, down the
columns and in and out of order clearly and quickly.

pull	from	long	scrap	fun
felt	jump	sock	on	hand
ten	string	red	have	rod
puppet	leg	run	with	can